OLD MAN DOTS

Helen Porteous & Linda Lycett

Children are the future
So teach them well and true
Enjoy book reading with them
and teach them all the words
so they can read the books themselves
or
read them back to you

Old Man Dots had a broken dot.

He wanted to take the torn spot off, and get a new one glued on. He could not use his wing until the spot was fixed.

He wandered along the path, looking for anyone who had new dots to spare, or who had extra dots they didn't want any more.

Old Dots was getting very tired.

And the broken dot kept getting loose. His legs were hurting and shaking so much, he decided to have a rest under a blade of grass.

After his rest, Old Dots started hobbling down the path again.

All he wanted was to find a new shiny dot.

Three young dots saw him coming, and they didn't want to be glued onto the back of an old bug, so they decided to run away and hide.

Two waiting brown dots said "Hello" to Old Man Dot, and said they would tell him where to find new dots. They showed him the direction of the nearest spot shop.

Old Dot was so tired; he didn't have the energy to choose a new dot just yet. So he had another rest.

He woke up and saw a kind looking pixie standing next to him. Pixie said he would help Mr Dot choose a new black dot. And he would help glue it into place.

A nearby spot shop had lots of dots! Pixie and Old Man Dot chose a nice round and shiny black spot. It was hard to choose because all the dots looked so good.

Pixie person carefully peeled off the old broken dot, and glued the new one into place on Old Man Dot's side. It really looked quite smart and very tidy.

The three young dots came out of hiding, and jumped for joy. They were happy for Old Dot and happy they could still run around the place.

Old Man Dot thanked the kindly Pixie person for helping him, and then he toddled down the path with the new spot shining in the sun.

Everyone had been so kind to an old bug, thought Old Man Dot. The world is a good place with all the kind creatures helping me. And Old Man Dot smiled a happy smile.

About the Authors

Helen lives in the Mallee region of Northern Victoria and has always been interested in reading, writing, drawing and having adventures of the magical kind. Helen's stories and artwork bring the books to life. Many thanks to the Mallee Artists Swan Hill for supporting the fun side of creating cute and curious creatures. Other published books are Sandy the Flipper Dragon – Rose Dog Books, and MARA–Balboa Press.

Linda lives near Sydney, NSW and loves reading and her crafts of spinning and designing. Her love of books has brought her to helping other authors publish their books, and through this to co-authoring the Little Leaf Books with Helen. Linda has three grown children and six grandchildren, who have also inherited her love of books.

Also by Authors

Fairy Folk Series

Fairy Folk and Other Strange Little Creatures

Fairy Folk and the Magical Helpers

Fairy Folk and Fantastic Friends